MAGNA CARTA - STOCKS

The beginners guide to stock trading made super simple!

Atlas Wright

Kindle Direct Publishing

kindle direct publishing

DISCLOSURE

Financial Advice Disclosure

The information provided in this book is for educational and informational purposes only. It is not intended as, and shall not be understood or construed as, financial advice.

Readers are advised to consult with a qualified financial advisor or professional before making any financial decisions. The author and publisher of this book are not responsible for any financial decisions or actions taken by readers based on the information provided in this book. All investments carry risks, and past performance is not indicative of future results. The financial markets can be unpredictable, and it is crucial to conduct thorough research and seek professional advice before making any investment decisions.

The author and publisher do not have any affiliation with specific financial institutions or products mentioned in this book. Any references made are for illustrative purposes only and do not constitute an endorsement or recommendation. The reader assumes full responsibility for their financial decisions and actions, and the author and publisher disclaim any liability for any loss or damage incurred directly or indirectly from the use of the information provided in this book.

Esteemed Reader,
I hope you come to see the idea of seeking financial protection
and empowerment, drawing a parallel between the historical
Magna Carta's aim to limit the power of the government and
this book's emphasis on the importance of financial education.
I encourage you to share the knowledge you acquire to our
family, friends, and future generations. Through our collective
acquisition of expertise in global economics and the stock
market, we can contribute to the overall growth and prosperity
of our nation and the market, benefiting us all.
Thank you for taking the time to invest in my book. I truly
appreciate your support and hope you find it enjoyable, insightful
and meaningful.
Sincerely, Atlas Wright

CONTENTS

"Knowing is not understanding."
- Charles Kettering

The Game

E ndless nights, scorching summer days, your body weary and your mind dulled from the grind of desk-bound or physically demanding labor. Hard work, dedication, and sacrifice are put into devoting our efforts for financial gain. Once acquired, we need to put it to work for us as our "employees" and get our money to "work" for us in return, But how? "Investing in the stock market is one avenue to consider". The most overheard or over spoken line of our time; a time where inflation is eating at our dollar value and with interest rates constantly rising, the pressing question for the novice investor here is – HOW do I start investing in the stock market?

It seems like the complexity of the financial system was deliberately created to discourage the average person, allowing the system to maintain an advantage over those who may not grasp the potential benefits of investing. For the beginner investor this poses a huge concern. There is an overwhelming array of terms, definitions and rules to trading that could easily intimidate, discourage or turn away a new investor.

Instead, many individuals resort to depositing their funds into banks, where their money depreciates in savings or checking accounts offering a meager average annual percentage yield (APY) of 0.03%. Consequently, their money loses value to inflation each year, while banks profit by investing these funds and reaping returns of 15% APY or more. It's quite striking how banks often offer minimal returns for storing your money with them, all the while utilizing those funds to bolster their own investments and capital, leveraging this advantage over the assumption that you might not be as well-versed in the intricacies of financial rules and strategies.

What you truly desire is to beat them at their own game. Understand the art of keeping your money in motion, using it to generate more wealth for yourself and safeguarding your dollar from inflation. I've organized this book as a guide, gently leading you from the fundamental concepts and gradually progressing towards more advanced techniques. In a nutshell, you will acquire all the necessary knowledge to reach these goals through stock market ventures. Keep in mind that anyone can enter the stock market, but not everyone possesses the necessary know-how. *Gaining this knowledge will lift a veil, revealing what was previously obscured by lack of understanding...*

CHAPTER 1

The Curtain Unravels

O ur Tale begins when a growing, prosperous corporation aims to expand and finance new projects. To fund these new ventures, it releases a specific number of 'shares' on the stock market for public investment. To better understand this concept, imagine the company being divided into individual pieces and made available in a market for anyone to purchase. As the company succeeds or encounters setbacks, your ownership stake may either appreciate or depreciate in value. Additionally, it can yield a profit for you, or conversely, lead to a loss. A multitude of individuals leverage these setbacks or newfound highs to their advantage, purchasing when the market is down and selling when it's at its peak - this is the fundamental concept of stock trading.

When you acquire a stock/share from a company, you possess a portion of its assets and earnings. This means if you hold a significant proportion of the company's total shares, you have an indirect influence over the company! Suppose company A issues 1000 shares to finance their new project. As a trader, you acquire 500 of their shares. In this hypothetical scenario, you would now possess 50% ownership of the company.

Now as much as we all want to; this doesn't mean

run into the corporate office of your chosen investment and start taking physical items because you own a percent of the company's shares. All it means when you own a corporation's stock is that you have ownership in its financial operations. Owning a significant amount of shares or even a small amount depending on the share can give you another added bonus - **voters rights. You will possess the authority to participate in significant company decisions, projects, and expansions through methods such as mail, video calls, or in-person meetings!** Being invited to these meetings is a valuable privilege and a great chance to learn more about what your investing in.

To acquire this portion of a company, you require a "middle man", which is your **brokerage – put simply, a distributor of stocks to the general public, as otherwise, you wouldn't have access to purchase them elsewhere.** Stocks are transferred from corporations to exchanges and then made available for purchase by brokerages. Another valuable perk is provided by the **SIPC, which stands for Securities Investor Protection Corporation. This government entity safeguards your shares and cash assets in your brokerage account in the event of your brokerage declaring bankruptcy.** It covers up to $250,000 in uninvested cash idling in the account, or up to $500,000 for both invested positions and cash losses. It's akin to FDIC insurance for banks, which safeguards your checking or savings accounts. In this case, it's tailored for a brokerage account holding your stocks and uninvested cash – a remarkable form of complimentary protection! However, it's crucial not to be misled into thinking that SIPC coverage will shield you from poor investment decisions. Its function is solely to step in if the brokerage facilitating your stock transactions encounters a failure.

Be sure to weigh out your brokerages, as each of them excel in their own areas or better yet, consider having accounts in multiple brokerages to diversify where you invest! To captivate your focus, I should slip in that this "piece" you own may generate a tidy return known as a **dividend - a periodic payment (monthly, quarterly, semiannually, or annually) received for owning and holding a share**, which we'll cover more in depth in chapter 4. This is why Owning stock is crucial for wealth-building. By purchasing the company's products and investing in its stock, you contribute to its growth. In return, both you and the company benefit from the resulting profits—a mutually beneficial cycle, *beautiful!*

Our wonderful market

When considering the stock market as a whole, it's not confined to a specific physical location for trading, although places like Wall Street are associated with it. It's better described as a global financial network, with traders worldwide engaging in the buying and selling of various stocks. While there are also options to invest in foreign stocks from other countries' markets, it's important to bear in mind that there may be transaction fees or additional charges.

Stocks are traded on **exchanges - which can be likened to grocery stores. Instead of goods like sugar and bread, these exchanges deal in stocks**. Each market has its own stock that its selling. For instance, a British corporation looking to expand, would list its stock on the LSE (London Stock

Exchange). While an American corporation would prefer to list their stock on either Nasdaq (United States exchange) or NYSE (New York Stock Exchange). As a result, these stocks are typically available for purchase only on the market they are listed on, unless they are global shares (able to trade at any exchange) or as previously mentioned, you're willing to incur additional fees for stocks foreign from where you trade.

So, what precisely do these exchanges monitor? Stock exchanges, or markets, keep tabs on **indexes - a sophisticated way of referring to a collection of stocks grouped together for organizational and tracking purposes.** As an Example, the Standard and Poor's 500 (S&P 500) is an index that monitors the performance of the leading 500 large companies in the United States, while DIJA (the Dow Jones Industrial Average) follows the top 30 **blue-chip companies** – 30 **leading enterprises with a proven track record of outstanding performance**. Whether you're interested in investing in large corporations, technology, grocery chains, loans/debts, or trusts, the options are extensive. There is always an index monitoring these sectors, so make sure to leverage them to your benefit.

What I'm trying to convey here is you can utilize an index to discern whether it's solely the specific company you're investing in that's experiencing a decline, or if it's actually the entire sector facing a downturn. If the entire sector is facing a downturn, then we can safely assume that it's something other than the market itself. Consider this scenario: if you're trading a stock listed in the S&P 500 index and the **positions (the shares you hold in that specific company)** are on a downward trend, you can cross-reference the stock's performance with that of the entire index.

This comparison allows you to identify any similarities in the decline. If there's no resemblance, then it suggests that the issue lies solely with the company you're investing in. Conversely, if the patterns align, it indicates that all 500 companies in the S&P 500 are undergoing a similar downturn. I did mention that factors beyond the market could come into play. What might potentially influence the entire market? Well, it's a daunting term: a **CRASH.**

Recess or Recession?

Before we delve into what might trigger such a downturn, First, some Looming questions about exchanges and the market overall. You might wonder, why is it crucial for me to grasp this information, and more importantly, how does it translate into benefits for me? Of course, one of the most important rules of trading... **Risk mitigation**. Also referred to as **Hedging - ensuring your stocks from a loss,** much like insuring your vehicle or home from accidents and natural disasters. Many investors overlook the risks and find themselves in investments that exceed their risk tolerance. This is a key reason why so many investors face losses in the market. In the upcoming chapters, we'll delve into the specific impacts on individual stocks. However, it's crucial to shift our attention to a greater threat to your overall investments - the economy. Understanding this and learning how to **profit** while on a market decline can be immensely advantageous!

When the stock market crashes, stock value drops because companies aren't making a profit. That's bad news, so how can we possibly gain from such a **bear/bearish (Low or**

declining) market? Allow me to clarify. When inflation surges, and our country accumulates excessive debt, both banks and the Federal Reserve will raise interest rates on loans- be it auto loans, home mortgages, credit cards, or general debt. This aims to encourage us - consumers, corporations and small businesses, to reduce our spending collectively, enabling us to gradually repay our national debt more swiftly.

This approach helps prevent further debt accumulation, which, in turn, will reduce interest rates meaning everyone has more money in their pockets to spend in the future. Now, the downside of this course of action is that corporations, small businesses and individuals will reduce spending while waiting for the economy's interest rates to lower. As a result, your stock may experience a prolonged period of depreciation until the economy rebounds, a process that could span from weeks to potentially even years (though less likely in modern times).

Picture a seesaw: one end represents the stock market and its components, including businesses and us, the individual investors. On the opposite side, we have Federal Interest rates and their components – banks and politicians. Therefore, when global economic interest rates go up, it has repercussions on businesses and individuals until the economy recovers. Alright, let's get straight to the point. When the balance tips in favor of the federal reserves and banks, one way to secure your portfolio is by putting your money into stocks that are tied to bonds, **commodities (gold, silver, etc.)** and/or any **debt instruments-Any financial investment associated with debt or loans.** Hopefully, you're beginning to connect some dots. This is because when banks raise interest rates, it affects various debt-based financial instruments, including federal bonds, treasury indexes (which are stocks linked to government investments), and even debt assets like home mortgages and corporate bonds. While this might not be geared towards very new investors, I'll briefly touch on a few debt instruments as a reference for when trading and economics become more familiar for you.

Bond Funds - Before delving into the specifics of bond funds, it's important to have a basic understanding of what bonds entail, so you can make informed investment decisions. A **bond represents a loan extended by YOU to either a government or a corporation seeking funds for their upcoming ventures**. Unlike stocks, where you acquire ownership in a company, with bonds, you are essentially extending a loan to the entity, be it a company or a government, depending on the type of bond.

Because you're lending them **capital(money)**, they are obligated to repay you with both the initially lent amount and additional interest - Similar to when we apply for loans for our homes or vehicles, but in this scenario, you are the one extending the loan. A **bond fund is a stock that invests in a "bundle" of different types of bonds** – Treasury bonds, municipal(state) bonds, gov agency bonds and corporate bonds etc. It's worth noting that in a market downturn, it's typically less advisable to invest in corporate bonds due to their elevated interest rates, which can increase the likelihood of a corporation **defaulting – that is, being unable to repay the loan**. In contrast, governments consistently possess financial resources, and the chances of them defaulting are slim to none.

Recall the seesaw analogy. When a market experiences a downturn due to inflation and increasing interest rates, the seesaw tilts in favor of the government, while corporations are on the other side. By allocating a portion of your portfolio to debt instruments, you're essentially shifting across to join the government's side – and the balance tips in your favor! In times of economic hardship, bonds tend to either maintain or increase in value. This is precisely why our grandparents frequently encouraged us to invest in bonds!

Pros

> Directly impacted by economic interest rates, it tends to excel during periods of high inflation and elevated interest rates

> Consistent interest payments to you in form of dividends

Cons

> There's no specific maturity date involved because you're not directly purchasing the bonds. Instead, you're investing in a company that in turn invests in government bonds, municipal bonds, or corporate bonds.

Balanced funds - Operate as a type of stock company that spread investments across a diverse array of assets, including debt, equities, and notably, commodities like precious metals. The name "balance" fund itself conveys its purpose. It signifies that the investment company strives for a 50/50 portfolio composition, with, for instance, 50 percent allocated to debt instruments and the remaining 50 percent to equity stocks. If the economy takes a downturn, the 50 percent invested in debt will act as a safeguard against potential losses in your other 50 percent in equity stocks. This serves as an effective hedging strategy!

Imagine investing in a seasoned trader who actively manages a large pool of stock, with capital contributed by numerous investors. Unlike regular stocks, there's an active portfolio manager making purchases and trades within the fund. Essentially, you're investing in someone who invests in stocks and commodities - a sort of Stockception. Setting aside the playful terminology, I'm mentioning balance funds because, especially during economic downturns, assets like gold and silver tend to retain their value more effectively than the American dollar, which can be eroded by inflation.

Individuals might choose to invest in gold as a way to preserve their wealth during a recession, fearing a decrease in the value of their dollars. Keep in mind that the more diverse your portfolio, the lower your risk level. It's never advisable to concentrate all your assets in a single investment.

pros

> Incorporates assets such as gold and silver.

> More diverse – less risk

> Active portfolio manager

Cons

> Investment funds managed actively by professionals usually involve associated fees and expenses, so be sure to do your research.

> When employing a hedging strategy with debt assets, it's important to note that in the event of a rapid economic

recovery, you may potentially "miss-out" on significant market upswings, as debt assets tend to lose value in a scenario of lower interest rates.

Inverse ETFS - Are not suitable for novice investors. They fall under the category of Leveraged ETFs, which we can delve into further in chapter 5. I'll only be making a brief mention of it for now. This approach is more aligned with equity trading rather than hedging. At its core, it's a fund that mirrors a market index. You're basically making a speculative "bet" (with the backing of numbers and research of course) - that the market will experience a downturn. If you're correct and it reaches the anticipated low (or close to it), you can realize substantial gains.

However, like opening pandoras box, it's worth noting that this strategy can also lead to significant losses if the market doesn't actually crash. This method aligns more with equity trading, focusing on profit generation rather than portfolio protection. While not a conventional safeguarding strategy, you could emerge in a favorable position while the economy faulters.

Pros

> Significant potential for profit margin increase - substantial gains.

Cons

> elevated risk - potential for significant losses.

I trust that you now have a better understanding and grasped some methods to shield your dollar from the impacts of inflation, as the saying goes – *Gas prices are so high... That even the coronavirus stopped traveling.*

CHAPTER 2

Secrets...

U rgent Update! Company A has recently acquired cutting-edge AI technology, leading to a remarkable 50% surge in shareholder margins! As a result, certain shareholders of Company A have now attained millionaire status. But the question remains: how did some of these individuals anticipate or predict this development? Furthermore, how can one gain confidence in their stock selection without solely relying on emotional or speculative factors? First and foremost, the market is inherently driven by emotions - mostly due to ignorance in investing. Allow me to illustrate with a real-world example: Consider a highly lucrative electric car company Tesla (TSLA).

Thanks to a yearly rise in revenue and a consistent reduction in the company's debt, Tesla (TSLA) is progressing well. In mid-July, the average stock price was around $244, with occasional highs reaching close to $260. Approximately on August 7th, surprising news broke out that the Chief Financial Officer of the company had resigned, catching many off guard. Shareholders hadn't yet had a chance to investigate the reasons behind this departure or scrutinize the company's annual revenue trends. Instead, they were unsettled by the sudden downturn, prompting them to opt for selling their shares...*Fear*.

As a result, the stock undergoes a bearish trend, with prices dropping to a low of $212. After a few weeks, it gradually recovers to its standard level around $244, and even surpasses it to $275.00 in the subsequent weeks as things stabilize. All of this unfolds within the time span of a month. But why did the stock price recover so soon? The market swing was driven purely by emotion. If shareholders had been more astute and utilized the correct resources and research methods, they would have discovered that the CFO's departure was due to personal reasons, and the company's financials were actually improving and stable.

Had they simply held onto their shares and waited for the emotional wave to subside, they wouldn't have incurred losses by selling during the dip. Instead, they would have seized the opportunity to capitalize on the upswing that followed. However, if the circumstances were different, for example, If the CFO had departed due to causing harm to the company's financials, and the succeeding CFO would need to rectify the situation, then the price would stay depressed for a period until the company's financials stabilize.

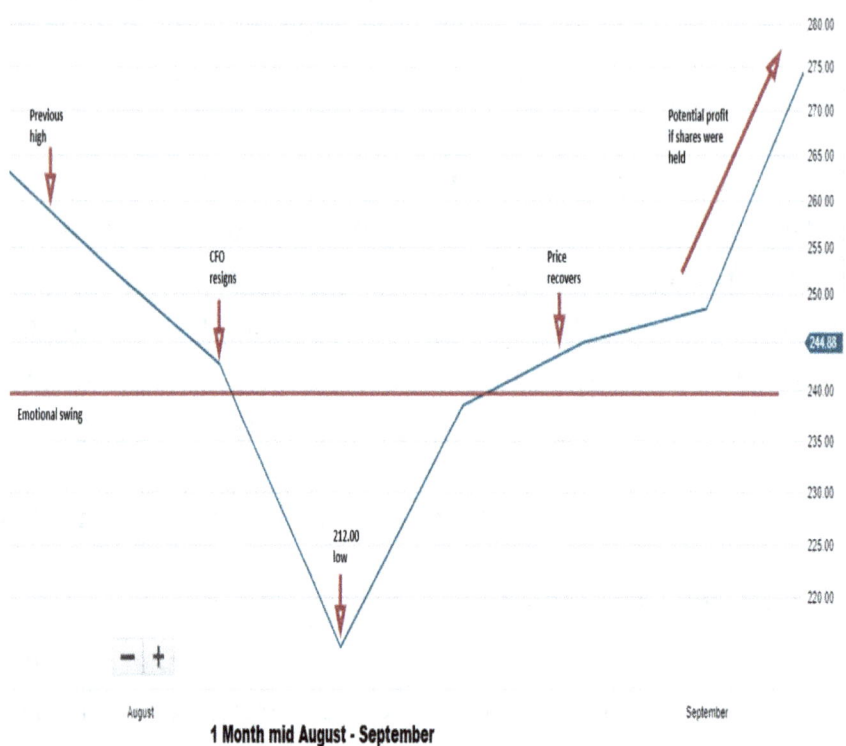

1 Month mid August - September

(TSLA) – TESLA

The central point I'm emphasizing here is that often, market movements are driven by speculation, regardless of the actual circumstances. A major factor in this situation is a lack of knowledge in conducting proper research or a deficiency in understanding. It's important to remember that not everyone comprehends the intricacies of stock investment. The ratio of professional investors to amateurs heavily favors in number by amateurs. Amateur investors typically base their stock research on emotions. Often turning to biased easy to access media sources that may promote fabricated or even purchased news. Alternatively, many individuals won't research and monitor the market altogether due to a lack of knowledge in this area.

Consequently, the entire market will be heavily swayed by emotion, sometimes overshadowing the importance of level-headed decision-making. We will explore some straightforward research techniques that may or may not be widely known, particularly in the realm of data research for stocks. These methods involve using both numerical data and leveraging "emotional" market swings to your advantage. This knowledge equips you with the ability to effectively monitor your stocks and discern reliable sources of information from biased ones. Conducting thorough research on your investments and staying updated with the right news and media sources will grant you with the confidence needed to securely hold stocks in your portfolio, alleviating the anxiety of potential fluctuations or loss. *Let's begin!*

In today's landscape, numerous stock research platforms and channels are available. However, discerning their credibility can be a challenge. Many cable TV news networks, as well as the advertisements or news articles that immediately appear when you open your internet browser, are often sponsored or biased. Media outlets are often influenced or controlled by corporations, which diminishes their reliability. Relying on social media or certain news networks for accurate information is akin to placing trust in sources that can be easily influenced by money.

Dependable sources present numerical data, assess risks and rewards associated with stocks, and provide forecasts for potential future profits. To expedite your search, consider utilizing these trustworthy news networks and apps. However, it's crucial for you to gauge the reliability of any source on your own. Establishing multiple sources is a recognized method for ensuring well-supported stock research. I want to clarify that I have no affiliation or endorsement from any of these companies. They simply hold personal significance for me. *Let the facts speak for themselves.*

Wall Street Journal – This is an incredibly reputable source that has been providing financial investment news and advice since 1889. It's truly remarkable. This resource is likely the most widely recognized and highly praised one out there. It offers forecasts, data, charts, and impressively swift news delivery. In the world of trading, having information at your fingertips is crucial because at any given moment, whether it's a minute, a day, or a week, your stock could experience significant movement, and having the edge in receiving information promptly is invaluable. Personally, if I had to pick just one, it would definitely be the Wall Street Journal. The only drawback I find with the Wall Street Journal is that to fully enjoy its services, you have to commit to a monthly or yearly subscription.

__Bloomberg__ – Similar to the Wall Street Journal, Bloomberg provides an extensive array of news encompassing financial politics and analytics. It's a source I find beneficial for cross-referencing, ensuring I don't miss any critical information. What sets Bloomberg apart is its software program that grants access to real-time global news—a valuable tool, especially for institutional investors. It's important to keep in mind that gaining entry to these invaluable resources usually involves a monthly or annual subscription.

__Internet advisor websites__ - lets tip toe carefully on this one. I'm talking about platforms such as Seeking Alpha or the Motley Fool. As I previously noted, the market can be significantly influenced by emotions, leading to many of its fluctuations seeming disconnected from financial fundamentals. If that's the scenario, I prefer utilizing sources aligned with emotional investing. Many of these less mainstream internet investment communities offer complimentary data and analytics, although you do have the option to pay for additional features. I frequently find valuable insights and perspectives on these platforms, though the reliability tends to be a mixed bag, typically a 50/50 outcome. While platforms of this nature have faced allegations of **market manipulation, involving the circulation of false positive/negative news to influence market prices**, they can still serve as a resource for cross-referencing emotional stock movements.

Embrace a different perspective – While This advice is aimed at broadening your approach to investment research in a more general sense, it's refreshing to gain a different perspective. Discover your unique way of gaining confidence in your stock. There's a tale of a billionaire oil tycoon who launched satellites into space to assess the reserves of various oil companies he was looking to invest in. He employed these satellites to gauge the size and quantity of their storage facilities, differentiating every company's oil reserves until he identified the most promising one. While it may just be a story, it serves as an inspiring example of how thinking outside the box can help transcend limitations.

Social media platforms - While not a reliable source, holds significant sway due to the trust people place in it. Utilizing the short-term emotional fluctuations in the market can be a means to capitalize on these rapid shifts for profit. It's also valuable as a benchmark when a stock's movement appears financially inexplicable. Consider, for instance, ET (Energy Transfer), an oil and pipeline energy company with an average share price of approximately $11.85 in a favorable year. Due to the global transition from oil to renewable resources, the company's year-to-year revenue was on a decline. However, Energy Transfer's strategic shift towards natural gas, a crucial element for advancing the renewable energy industry, encouraged investors to take a substantial gamble, leading to a surge in prices to $13.80.

Despite the company's less favorable financial metrics, the stock continues to experience an increase in value and maintains its position... It's truly relying on optimism and future projections. *We should seize this opportunity to ride the volatile upswings, but also be ready to sell when reality sets in, revealing that hope alone isn't enough, and only concrete facts will sustain long-term gains.*

Concrete facts!

Setting aside emotional and media-driven research, let's turn our attention to concrete facts. Specifically, I'm talking about numbers. When it comes to stock analysts, advisors, and professional traders, how do they obtain access to a company's financial data? Is there a special privilege granting them the ability to view a company's total assets and debt? The answer is straightforward: anyone can obtain this information, provided they know where to look. You won't reliably find details like company revenues, debt, net and gross income, or even their assets (both stocks and physical) through a simple Google search.

This might appear to be information that requires extensive research to uncover, but it's actually quite accessible. Similar to how we, as individuals, have to report our income to the government at the end of the year for taxes, the process works in a similar manner for companies. However, because individuals have a stake in these companies (through ownership of shares), the companies are obligated to release annual forms that present revenue, net income, and overall financials - essentially, everything you need to know as a shareholder. These forms are referred to as **SEC filings. Financial documents that any business selling shares is required to submit to the government and listed for the public**

to see on an annual or semi-annual basis, depending on the type of business and form.

These documents offer in-depth financial details about the company, encompassing annual operating revenues, net income, outstanding debts, liabilities, as well as the number of **subsidiary(secondary)** companies it possesses. This information is openly accessible to the public and serves as a crucial tool for analysts to assess a company's year-to-year performance, evaluating its strengths, weaknesses, and progress. Whenever a major event occurs within a company, it is imperative that this information be made public. If a CEO or CFO resigns, it is a legal requirement for the company to disclose this information to the public, as stakeholders hold a vested interest in the company. Another instance of this is **insider trading, which involves trading among high-ranking individuals within an institution, such as directors, CFOs, and CEOs.**

These filings will detail the precise amounts involved in these insider trades, including the number of shares they either sold or purchased. This is tremendously beneficial for us as investors, as it safeguards us against a corporation providing false information about its financial status to its stakeholders. Furthermore, it enables us to expose any unlawful insider trading intended to manipulate the market, such as a CEO rapidly divesting all of their stock just before news of the company's failure becomes public. Remember the importance of risk mitigation? Well, as you can see it applies to your research efforts as well. This is where confidence is established, and profits start to flow - through research!

There are numerous types of SEC forms, but I'll cover

the key ones you need to be familiar with for analyzing a company's financials and movements. To find these forms visit the **U.S. Securities and Exchange Commission website or simply search EDGAR: company filings.** I'll give you a brief overview, as it's important for you to develop the ability to independently interpret these forms. You've been equipped with the necessary resources and knowledge, it's up to you to invest the effort.

Form 10k – This document is an essential annual requirement for corporations. It serves as the centerpiece and core source of financial information. Within it, you will discover a comprehensive overview of a company's financial status. While delving into it might seem daunting, it's crucial to emphasize that you should primarily concentrate on the total annual revenues, juggle total debts and liabilities against yearly net income, and voilà, you'll have a fundamental report of the company's annual net income – the residual profit left after all taxes, operational expenses, debts, and costs have been settled. By comparing this data with the previous year's information, and continuing this process over time, you start to establish the foundation for confidence when it comes to holding, selling, or buying shares. *Feeling more grounded?*

Form 8k- When a company reveals significant events like bankruptcies, substantial asset transactions, or executive changes, they are required to publicly disclose this information through this form. Within it lies a treasure trove of data crucial for informing your decision on whether to hold, buy or sell a stock. These kinds of changes can have a noticeable impact on stock prices, influenced by "emotion". It's crucial to use this information to your advantage and navigate through the emotional fluctuations with astuteness and composure.

Schedule 13d – Picture this: a group of high-profile, multi-millionaire investors locked in a fierce battle for control over a corporation's shares. It's important to remember that possessing shares equates to wielding indirect influence over a company. Given the substantial stake these individuals hold, they're vying for dominance to steer the company in their preferred direction. At this juncture, there are two potential outcomes: a favorable acquisition, where the company willingly embraces a premium offer from a prospective buyer; conversely, there's the less desirable scenario where a company seeks to acquire another against its will, amassing sufficient stocks to tilt the equity of the target company.

They achieve this also by persuading shareholders to cast proxy votes to remove the existing management and install a biased leadership chosen by the acquiring company. In the case of a beneficial acquisition, being aware of this can be advantageous. This is because stocks typically experience a significant price surge when acquired by a prosperous and established company. The Schedule 13D filing provides information about the percentage of shares acquired by one corporation from another corporation.

The field of stock research techniques is continuously evolving. Stay committed to your research to stay current with the market. The tactics outlined here serve as a foundation.

Keep exploring for improved methods; you might possess insights that lead you ahead of the curve, discovering strategies before they become widely known. *Don't forget to give your notes some note-able attention!*

CHAPTER 3

Let's Trade!

F inally, let's start trading, shall we? Bear with me here because the various approaches a trader can take in this regard can be quite... intricate. This is being mentioned with caution because in reality, it's quite easy to incur losses in trading when you just jump in and learn from experience. As a novice with limited capital, treating trading like a job can be risky. The learning curve in this field can result in financial losses. However, it's important to note that there are certain aspects of trading stocks that can only be truly grasped through firsthand experience.

To compound the challenge, some individuals tend to dive into exceedingly technical aspects, which can be overwhelming for a newcomer in trading. Not to worry, I'll share some tips in a sequence that simplified my understanding and eased me into stock trading. In my humble opinion, it's perilous to hastily engage in trading without a firm grasp of these three crucial aspects: understanding the different types of trading, knowing which stocks to consider, and familiarizing oneself with basic technicalities like charts and patterns.

After comprehending these three concepts, you can integrate them to mitigate risks and start generating profits.

Think of it as that initial push on a swing – once it's set in motion, the swing's momentum does the rest of the work.

Trading Types

Whether you're someone who enjoys generating income consistently, occasionally, or prefers to accumulate funds over time before making a sale, there's an investment strategy for every type of investor. In fact, you can even explore a combination of these approaches! Here are a variety of trading styles for you to delve into.

Scalping - A type of day trading and not to be confused with the traditional Native American "haircut", is a contemporary term used to describe the act of purchasing or selling an item at a price that deviates from its typical market value. While this concept is applicable in various sales scenarios, in the context of stocks, scalpers maintain positions for only a matter of **minutes or even seconds**.

They capitalize on exceedingly swift price fluctuations, making profits that may range from mere pennies to occasionally dollars. You might be wondering; how can someone turn a profit or be effective in this approach if they're essentially trading all day for just small gains? Well, there are several factors at play. It demands intense concentration and vigilant monitoring of market movements on a minute-to-minute basis. In addition, these traders have the advantage of utilizing tools like AI, applications, or other resources that aid in predicting, tracking, as well as executing buy and sell orders. Accuracy is absolutely crucial in this trading approach, as a mere lapse of minutes or even seconds can mean forfeiting a valuable opportunity.

Additionally, traders in this style typically operate with an even more substantial capital because the profits from each individual share's movement are so modest. This necessitates a sizable sum of money to effectively generate a meaningful profit. However, it's important to note that having a larger capital base also entails a higher potential for both gains and losses. Here's an example: Let's say you're trading shares of Company A, holding a total of $20,000.00 in shares valued at $10.20 each. Within two minutes, the stock price rises to $10.40. You decide to sell your entire position, resulting in a profit of 20 cents per share. Doing the calculation, with $20,000 worth of shares at $10.20 apiece, you would have approximately 1960 shares. At a profit of 20 cents per share, this translates to a gain of $392 in just two minutes.

You can see here how a highly skilled scalper can earn significant profits in an extremely brief period. You must possess a certain level of confidence and financial stability because managing such a substantial amount of money within a short timeframe is a significant endeavor, and many individuals struggle with the pressure it entails. *It's even quicker than some other endeavors, if you catch my drift!*

Pros

> Gain from mere seconds to minutes!

> If done correctly and consistently, this can evolve into a primary source of income, there is no limit how much one can make per hour!

Cons

> For a beginner investor, this strategy demands an extraordinarily high capital investment in single or multiple shares, which can be exceptionally risky. Typically, experience in trading is necessary before delving into this type of approach.

> It's highly challenging/impossible to make accurate predictions given the limited time frame of seconds or minutes, as there isn't substantial research to support such rapid decisions.

> To excel in this style of investing, one needs a significant array of additional tools like AI, computers, software, and tracking apps to become efficient.

> Requiring a high level of focus and emotional control during rapid market fluctuations, resisting the urge to sell out of fear can be quite demanding.

General day trading – Day traders hold their positions for varying durations, spanning from **hours down to mere seconds, but they never extend beyond a single day**. They strategically capitalize on price fluctuations during distinct busy periods of the market, such as the opening, midday, and closing hours. However, come the end of the trading day, a day trader sells off all of their positions and refrains from holding any stock overnight. The reason for this is that keeping positions overnight can be quite risky if you're aiming for swift profits on a day-to-day basis.

A stock's price can experience significant fluctuations overnight due to news or unforeseen events. This applies to weekends as well when the market is closed. A day trader necessitates a substantial starting capital to potentially realize considerable profits. While not on the same scale as a scalper, it's still a noteworthy amount to navigate the more significant price shifts that can amount to several dollars per hour rather than mere cents per second or minute. Day traders rely on applications to assist in efficient stock tracking and trading. Given the fast-paced nature of their work, using programs that implement stop limits or trailing stops is essential for precision in buying and selling.

While day trading demands quick decisions within limited time frames, successful practitioners don't rely solely on chance or emotions. They frequently employ technical analysis, delving into charts and patterns to make well-informed forecasts about price movements. Additionally, some may integrate fundamental analysis to gauge a company's financial standing and market conditions. Emotions can indeed come into play, particularly for less experienced traders.

However, seasoned day traders make it a priority to uphold discipline and adhere closely to their strategies. They often establish specific entry and exit points based on their analysis to mitigate the impact of emotions. To sum up, day trading entails uncertainty, but it's not solely dependent on luck or sentiment. It necessitates a blend of proficiency, tactics, and a deep understanding of the market.

Pros

> Consistent revenue stream if executed correctly – (could

become primary source of income)

> Substantial profit potential

> Avoid overnight and weekend risks

Cons

> High-risk endeavor with limited research opportunities due to the single-day timeframe. It necessitates a focus on patterns and chart analysis, or entering with prior knowledge of how the stock may perform throughout the week you're trading.

> Requires Effective risk management and comprehending the stock you're investing in, being attuned to both emotional and financial trends.

> It's important to research and be aware that many brokerages may have transaction fees or specific rules regarding same-day buying and selling of shares.

Swing trading – The *magnum opus*, my current favored approach to trading, strapping in your position at the dip and riding that profit margin all the way up. Great for investing during emotional swings, seizing opportunities during market dips and taking the upswing back to the peak, then repeating the process – it's an elegant strategy. In contrast to day traders, swing traders retain their positions for a span of **several days to a few weeks.**

Maintaining positions for these durations can prove highly beneficial. It provides ample time for thorough research, ensuring a strong foundation for your trading decisions. Here's an example: Atlas has been closely monitoring company A's stock for his swing trading strategy for week, Atlas purchases 100 shares of Company A at $13.00 per share. Having a grasp of the day-to-day or week-to-week patterns of Company A, he spots a developing opportunity. The stock subsequently climbs by $10.00 to reach $23.00 per share. In this scenario, Atlas has generated a profit of $1,000.00 from his ownership of 100 shares, all within the span of roughly a week.

Additionally, it opens up more potential for profit, albeit with added risk for bearish investors when holding overnight or over the weekend. However, for bullish investors, if the market moves in their favor overnight or the weekend, the gains can be even more significant. Imagine you entered the market at the start of an upward trend and you've gained $10. In contrast, a day trader who closes all their positions by the end of the day would have also made $10. However, if you choose to hold your position overnight, and the next day the stock sees another $10 increase, your total gain would now be $20. See how this strategy can be highly beneficial under favorable market conditions? Furthermore, it doesn't demand constant monitoring and trading. Just a few days at a time, which makes it ideal as a supplementary endeavor alongside your primary source of income. It has the potential to generate additional income ranging from hundreds to even thousands – let your imagination be your guide.

Keep in mind to closely monitor the stock for a span of weeks to days when engaging in swing trading. It's crucial to thoroughly comprehend the optimal entry point (using charts and patterns) to maximize profit potential or to mitigate substantial losses before establishing your position. I prefer selecting a handful of companies for swing trading - I tend to focus on high-volume trading stocks that display significant volatility. This is because their substantial price fluctuations within a short timeframe translate to greater profit potential for me and the substantial number of shares in circulation indicates that the stock is frequently traded, making it readily convertible to cash and less prone to prolonged dips. Then, observing them closely over a few weeks to acquaint myself with their patterns and daily movements.

After gaining familiarity, I choose one company to enter, ride the upward swing, sell, and then use the profits to transition into another company. This allows me to capitalize on opportunities while waiting for the previously invested company to experience a dip. - It's a fantastic cycle - while one company is experiencing a dip, I'm riding the upward momentum of another. And when the first one starts to dip, I switch back to the other. This strategy allows for a continuous flow of opportunities and potential gains. But... how do I determine the right moments to buy or sell? - Don't worry, we'll cover this in detail in the section on charts and patterns.

The allure of swing trading is especially pronounced for novice investors with limited capital. Depending on their research and analysis, they have the potential to achieve substantial gains through this approach. You mainly capitalize on short-term emotional shifts in the market, which underscores the value of tapping into media and sources skilled at shaping public sentiment. Remember our discussion on how emotions drive market dynamics? Well, this becomes your tool to capitalize on those rapid and erratic swings, all before the shares revert to their average price or stage a recovery. In the regular ebb and flow of share prices, you keep an eye out for a unique opportunity or a discernible pattern to emerge. This is where you pinpoint your entry point, and *here is where you unearth your buried treasure…*

Pros

> Achieving goals becomes more manageable due to the extended time intervals between trades.

> Trading requires a smaller amount of capital! Compared to day trading.

> Requires far fewer technical resources compared to day trading.

Cons

> Conducting thorough monitoring and analysis before making a purchase is essential.

> Emotional swings in the market can be highly irrational, to the point where even technical analysis may not suffice.

> There's a possibility of missing out on substantial long-term returns. For instance, if you're constantly swinging a stock and it consistently climbs week after week, you might find yourself consistently buying in at high points and selling prematurely, when you could have opted for a position trading strategy instead.

Position trading

"The conventional approach to trading"

The general "overall" way of trading. Most market participants engage in position trading, whether they realize it or not. This involves holding shares for **months to**

years, capitalizing on long-term gains without the day-to-day burden of constant research and analytics—although it's still necessary, just not as frequently. I find position trading to be personally advantageous for various reasons. However, it's important for you to weigh the pros and cons of position trading and form your own opinion based on the information here. For starters, if you're already occupied with a 9-5 job, aiming to build your capital, position trading offers a convenient approach.

It doesn't require constant monitoring at your computer or the need to decide whether to actively watch the market on a given day. Position trading is particularly welcoming to novice investors, as it tends to be more forgiving of losses. Since you're holding positions for the long term, any short-term setbacks are typically regained over time. The beauty of position trading lies in the fact that you don't require a substantial amount of capital to begin. If you're considering day trading in the future but need to accumulate funds more rapidly, holding a position in a well-known, reputable company that you've thoroughly researched and have an emotional attachment to can be a lucrative strategy.

It has the potential to grow into a more significant portion of your portfolio, possibly in the near future. Conducting thorough research and analyzing the stock's long-term trends is imperative before making an investment, as you're essentially wagering on the company's long term sustained success. To offer a different perspective, numerous individuals maintain long-term investments in major S&P 500 and Dow Jones index companies. Together, they collectively represent the entirety of the United States market, encapsulated by the

NASDAQ index. Viewed collectively, investing in these shares essentially amounts to a wager on the long-term performance of the entire United States market, which hinges on economic conditions. Why?

Because these encompass sizable, dependable, and profitable companies with longstanding track records, attesting to their sustainability. When you hold shares in large companies that essentially drive the entire economy, your risk naturally diminishes significantly. For instance, if you invested a modest $5000 in WMT (Walmart) in the year 2000, that investment would be worth approximately $18,600 today. Here lies a significant drawback - time. It's the foremost adversary in position trading. While it's possible to recover from a substantial financial loss, the time spent cannot be regained...

Pros

> If you have a packed schedule, position trading can be your ally!

> Accruing substantial long-term returns with a modest initial investment.

> Reduced reliance on technology, less time commitment, and lower stress levels if executed properly.

Cons

> Once time passes, it cannot be recovered, even if the shares experience a future drop, erasing all gains accumulated over the years.

> Commonly, individuals have a tendency to retain their positions even when they are significantly overvalued. Rather than selling, greed often takes over, compelling them to hold

on with the expectation that the shares will continue to rise. However, they may eventually revert to their average price, causing a missed opportunity to capitalize on an emotional shift in the market.

> Over the long term, a multitude of events can unfold, potentially impacting your shares. Effective management of your research is paramount in navigating these situations.

Above all, it's crucial to remember that there's no one-size-fits-all approach to trading. The most effective method depends entirely on your schedule and lifestyle—choose what suits you best!

STOCK TYPES

The heart and soul of trading lies in the shares we invest in, as they are the engine behind our gains. I like to view it with a touch of imagination - I'm essentially selecting where to send my money to work for me - but the selection of stocks can be a daunting task. Does the type really make a difference, and what do these classifications imply? With such a vast array of options for investment, it's a genuine challenge to discern where to allocate resources effectively. Here, we'll address these questions in a straightforward manner, by dissecting various types of stocks, explaining why some individuals choose to trade them, and outlining their trading approaches.

Stocks/Equities

(Explained in chapter 1) Stocks are often referred to as equities, reflecting the fact that by owning shares, you technically co-own a portion of the company. Equity stocks are essentially shares that you trade at their **face value or their initial purchase price**. When you trade a stock like Walmart (WMT), if you purchase a share at $105.00 and later sell it for $150.00, you're trading for its equity, or in simpler terms, you're buying and selling a piece of ownership in the company. Simple, yet there are many subcategories when it comes to equity shares. One catagory that should definitely be touched on is **foreign stock**.

So far the U.S. currently accounts for over 50 percent of the worlds market, but not for long. Many markets around the world are continually expanding and growing at a rate much faster than the United States. With many countries outsourcing labor and material, it's only a matter of time before the market balances out towards these emerging markets. When investing in foreign stocks, it's important to consider the potential impact of significant foreign transaction fees associated with currency exchange between countries. To mitigate these costs, investors often turn to **Depository Receipts, financial instruments that represents shares of foreign companies**. These instruments enable investors to trade foreign company shares on thier local stock exchange without navigating the complexities of cross-border transactions.

Examples of Depository Receipts include American Depository Receipts (ADRs) or Chinese Depository Reciepts (CDRs), among others. These Receipts are either **sponsored** or **unsponsored**. Sponsored Depository Receipts grant investors the same ownership rights as those in the home country of the purchased shares, even if they are in a different country. In contrast, unsponsored Depository Reciepts may not offer the same rights as the home country holder, so typically going for a sponsored company is the smart choice to make. Investing in foreign shares offers maximum diversification, a crucial strategy in safeguarding against economic downturns. This diversification proves beneficial in times of economic crisis, as poor performance in one country's economy can be offset by investments in another country experiencing growth.

Its important to note that each country operates under distinct laws and regulations, which can significantly impact stock values. For instance, consider China's ecommerce boom, where shareholders invested in CDRs linked to booming ecommerce companies during the surge of affordable ecommerce to the U.S. However, because China is a communist country, as these companies expanded, government intervention occurred, stalling their growth and diminishing the stock value. This underscores the necessity of understanding the economic landscape and a country's situation before committing to investments. Being informed about the economic climate and legal framework helps investors make more strategic and resilient choices in their portfolio managment.

Stock Funds

In broad terms, the term "fund" refers to gathering money and using it for a specific purpose. When it comes to stock funds, the principle remains quite similar. Stock funds involve a collective pool of money contributed by investors, such as yourself and me. This pool is then managed by an investment firm or broker, which allocates the funds into a diverse range of stocks, bonds, or other assets, depending on the specific investment objectives in place.

Funds are essentially a bundle of stocks traded as a unified entity. This means you don't have to individually purchase each stock within the bundle, and it also provides you with exposure to diversity. Consider this: rather than acquiring numerous individual stocks to diversify your investments, why not obtain them all in a bundled package at a discounted rate? This way, you can gain exposure to various sectors of the market, reducing potential losses and potentially increasing your gains. The primary purpose of funds is to serve as a safety net, primarily through diversification.

When you invest in any type of "fund" — whether it's a mutual fund, ETF, or bond fund — it's important to understand that you don't own each stock inside that fund separately. Essentially, you're investing in a company that, in turn, invests in a broad and diversified portfolio of stocks. As this portfolio of stocks generates profits, you, in turn, receive a percentage of those gains – since you paid just a percentage of the premium for the positions in that fund. It's important to note that funds can be focused on a single sector, such as the technology sector, where the portfolio invests in various technology companies. Alternatively, they can be diversified across multiple sectors, like medical and technology, with investments in several companies within each sector.

In contrast to equity stocks, funds fall into two categories: actively managed and not actively managed. Actively managed funds (e.g., mutual funds) are overseen by a dedicated fund manager who specializes in the buying and selling of shares within the portfolio. On the other hand, not actively managed funds (e.g., ETFs) lack a fund manager actively involved in trading the shares in that portfolio. This means that if the shares within the portfolio decrease in value, there won't be anyone actively managing it to sell and potentially reinvest in more profitable assets- on the other hand you won't have to pay fees.

One final point to note is that funds are typically bought and sold differently compared to individual stocks. Due to their nature as a package of stocks, bonds and commodities they are not usually traded day-to-day like stocks, but rather intended for longer-term holding. Given the diverse range of options within funds, allow me to introduce you to some widely recognized examples.

Mutual Funds

Regarding mutual funds, it's a term that's frequently used in investing discussions, sometimes not entirely accurately due to its widespread usage. Personally, it irks me when I hear the phrase "just invest in mutual funds" being casually thrown around to new investors. This is bothersome for one main reason . It's an overly broad statement, akin to saying "just drink water if you're thirsty" – when in fact, there's a distinction between saltwater, which could be harmful, and purified, safe-to-drink water.

Mutual funds encompass a diverse range of funds, including Index funds, balance funds (as mentioned in Ch.1), bond funds (as mentioned in Ch.1), income funds, and more. The list is extensive. What's crucial is comprehending the term in its entirety. At its core, a mutual fund is essentially a substantial pool of funds contributed by investors like you and me. This pool is not limited to investments solely in stocks; it also includes various other assets, such as gold, trusts, and essentially anything of value or considered an asset. What's particularly beneficial is that these funds play a significant role in managing your 401k or IRA accounts. Do you see the broader perspective now?

This collection of stocks and commodities serves as a means to access other assets beyond the stock market, providing a hedge for the investments you have within the stock market. This approach shields you from exclusively focusing on stock investments, as you essentially have a stake in various assets globally. For instance, let's say I aim to diversify my investments and allocate a portion of my funds to gold, but I prefer not to physically store it at home. In this scenario, I would opt to invest in a mutual fund that includes holdings in both stocks and gold investments. This is just a straightforward example of how mutual funds can provide exposure to various assets without the need for physical possession.

It's quite satisfying, knowing that you can own certain assets around the world without the hassle of travel and its expenses. It's also worth noting that mutual funds can be either actively managed or passively managed, so it's important to investigate this aspect before selecting your fund. Furthermore, the process of buying and selling these is distinct in the market. You're essentially investing in a company that, in turn, invests in these assets. Therefore, you can't simply buy and sell them on a day-to-day basis like you would with individual equity shares.

ETF – Exchange Traded Funds

let's break down these concepts using the terms we've covered. We'll begin with "E" for Exchange. As we discussed in chapter one, exchanges can be likened to grocery stores. While grocery stores handle goods like sugar and bread, exchanges deal in stocks. Therefore, these funds are traded on exchanges in a similar manner to how stocks are traded. Moving on to "T" for traded. Unlike mutual funds, ETFs can be traded on a daily basis, similar to individual stocks. This is because they are invested in a bundle of highly liquid equity shares, which means they can be easily bought or sold in the market. The "F" is for Funds. This term refers to the basket or package of stocks or commodities that we have chosen to invest in.

Many individuals prefer trading ETFs because their price movements are generally less volatile compared to holding shares in an individual company, but more volatile than a mutual funds price movement. What sets an ETF apart from other funds is that its face value fluctuates daily, similar to a stock, unlike a mutual fund. Additionally, it won't be significantly impacted if a single company within the ETF's extensive portfolio experiences a significant drop in value. Moreover, funds frequently follow indexes, a concept we discussed in Chapter 1. Indexes serve as a sophisticated method of organizing and tracking a group of stocks for analytical purposes. Much like the S&P 500, which means, looking at the bigger picture – you're invested in the top 500 companies in the USA, without having to pay the substantial premium you would incur if you were to individually purchase all the stocks in that portfolio.

This makes ETFs an attractive option for many investors! A notable real-world instance of an ETF index fund is (VOO) the VOO S&P 500 ETF index fund. Managed by Vanguard (investment company), the fund's primary goal is to mirror the performance of the 500 major companies in the United States. Once you grasp the concept, it becomes much simpler. "VOO" stands for Vanguard, "S&P 500" denotes the top 500 companies being monitored by Vanguard and ETF is the type of stock – an exchange traded fund. *Upon gaining a clear understanding, it becomes apparent that the entire framework is remarkably uncomplicated.*

Charts

Analyzing stock charts, is a relatively straightforward task. Observing the current price (face value), trading volume (amount of trades made in a particular session, use this to gauge the popularity of a stock), and movement (volatility) is readily discernible. Put simply, reading a general stock chart and understanding how it works is very easy. However, what I'd like to emphasize is the significance of using candlestick charts. Why? Regular line charts lack the capability to indicate the market's opening and closing prices for the day, unlike candlestick charts. Understanding this distinction is crucial for investors. As mentioned earlier, it aids in determining optimal entry and exit points during market swings, forming a strategic approach to identify the right moments to buy or sell. Once you grasp its fundamentals, reading a candlestick chart becomes an easy task.

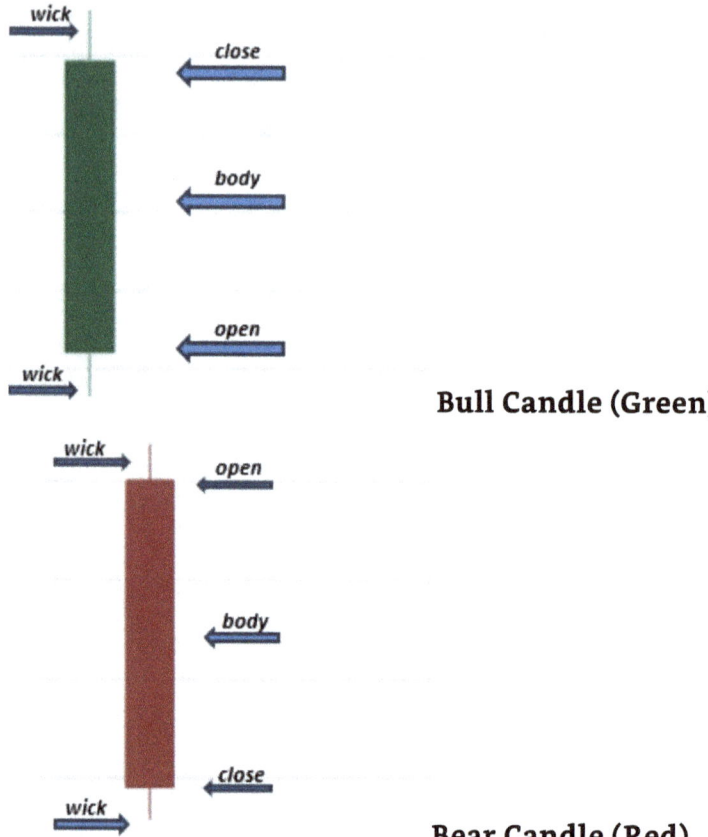

Bull Candle (Green)

Bear Candle (Red)

The green candlestick, also known as a bull candle, or the red candlestick, referred to as a bear candle, represents a specific day, week, or month (depending on your chosen time frame setting). A green candlestick indicates that the market traded higher than its previous time frame (bullish), while a red candlestick denotes trading lower than the prior time frame (bearish). On a bull candle, the **top end** signifies the day's closing price, while on a bear candle, it indicates the day's opening price.

The **lower end** of a bull candle represents the day's opening price, whereas on a bear candle, it stands for the day's closing price. Depending on whether the day, week, or month traded higher or lower than the preceding period, the bull and bear candles will alternate, as they are inherently opposing indicators. The **body** of the candlestick illustrates the average range of price fluctuations within that designated timeframe. Extending from both ends of the candlestick are slender lines known as **wicks or shadows**, signifying the complete span of price movement during that period of time. Of course, real-world examples often make explanations clearer. Here's another one for you – Atlas, the day trader, has been diligently analyzing candlestick charts for Company A.

Through his observations, he's identified a recurring pattern: Company A tends to open 2 percent lower than its previous day's closing price before eventually reverting to its average price for that day. Capitalizing on this insight, Atlas strategically places a buy order set at 2 percent below the average price during the opening the next day. As anticipated, the stock exhibits this pattern, fluctuating back to its usual price and even surpassing it. This well-informed move proves advantageous for Atlas in his trading strategy. Atlas not only capitalized on his foresight regarding the market's lower opening but also garnered additional profits from the gains achieved later in the day. *Voila!* By utilizing the candlestick charts open and close data, Atlas was able to capitalize on the stocks movement.

Now, let's simplify the understanding of one of the most crucial aspects of chart analysis: **supports, resistances, and identifying the current average price.** While some investors tend to overcomplicate this, I prefer to keep it as straightforward/simple as possible. Depending on whether you're engaged in day trading, swing trading, or positions trading, you'll want to strategically plot your lines to align with your specific timeframe goals. By plotting these three lines on your chosen chart, you'll be equipped to pinpoint secure entry and exit points for your trading strategies.

The **resistance line, often likened to a ceiling, marks the highest price the stock has reached within your specified trading timeframe, yet has not managed to exceed.** When ceilings are on the verge of being breached, it's customary that if they are, a new benchmark or support line for the stock is established. This implies that the price generally won't regress unless there's a significant external event or development. The **average line represents the mean price at which the stock is currently being traded.** This serves as your safety indicator, giving you a clear signal of whether the price is favorable for selling or buying. Lastly, the **support line designates the lowest point the stock has reached within that timeframe, but has not fallen below.** Usually, when a stock falls below a support level, the corresponding ceiling will also decrease, reverting to the stock's previous support and ceiling levels. This demonstrates the interconnected nature of these key price points.

Here, I have provided a graph from a real world scenario, to illustrate how graphing these 3 essential lines shielded me from a significant market decline, leading to substantial gains thereafter.

This is a genuine scenario that I'd like to share for its illustrative value. Before delving into this example, it's important to note that I conducted both factual and emotional research on the company. This was crucial in deciding where to plot its support and average price. Understanding its present trend was the key to accurately establishing these points. For the sake of this example, let's refer to this stock as Company X. The chart previously shown covers a duration of approximately 8 months, with candlesticks representing each day. Given my intention to hold onto my shares for a few months, I decided to plot it for the current month, encompassing the preceding few months as well. The 3 lines spanning across the chart horizontally are your support, resistance and average lines.

The **purple** line serves as the **ceiling**, denoting the highest price reached by Company X. This was readily identifiable, as it reached an impressive high of nearly $280.00 over the course of these 8 months. Reaching and challenging this ceiling is pivotal for the stock to attain its next potential peak and establish a new support level. A breakthrough of this ceiling signals the potential for a new phase of heightened gains and potentially increased trading volume for the stock. In essence, it indicates a more robust and successful performance overall!

The **orange** line represents the **support** level. In May, Company X found itself in a trending sector of the market and established a new support or foundation. It's noticeable that the stock experienced significant drops twice within that 8-month period to its support line, but didn't go below the established support line. This suggests that the stock has a robust foundation at its current elevated price, indicating a level of stability and confidence in its value.

The red line in the middle signifies the stock's prevailing **average** price for that specific period, which stands at approximately $250.00. This line holds significant importance for investors, serving as a reference point for determining their buy or sell decisions. Simply put, if you conduct transactions between the support and the average line, or between the average line and the resistance, you are typically safeguarded against substantial losses. It's a practical guideline for making trading decisions.

Here's an example to illustrate this: Let's say you buy in at August on the chart at $230.00. You're shielded from a sudden significant loss because you're so close to the stock's support at $214.00. This means you'd only incur a maximum stop loss of $16 per share before the stock starts to recover. On the upside, if the stock were to rebound to the average price of $250.00 at the time you bought it, you'd make a profit of $20 per share. It's akin to having a safety net that works in two ways – one, to protect your shares in case of a sudden downturn, and the other, to ride the upswing for potential gains!

The last pointers are the two circles that highlight the prime times to buy in for maximum gains with Company X and arrows that show the potential gains. This is also a great time to introduce **stop losses, a stop loss acts as a safety measure for your investments in the stock market. When you set a stop loss, you're instructing your broker to automatically sell/buy your shares if the stock price reaches a specific level.** For instance, if you purchase a stock at $50 per share and want to limit potential losses, you might establish a stop loss at $45. If the stock price falls to $45 or below, your broker will execute the sale to minimize your losses – As you can observe, with the implementation of stop losses, your loss was limited to $5. Without the use of stop losses, your loss would have exceeded $5.

This tool is valuable for risk management and safeguarding your investment. However, it's important to note that while a stop loss can help mitigate significant losses, it doesn't guarantee that you won't incur any losses. In rapid market declines, your shares may be sold at a slightly lower price than your stop loss threshold. You can also implement **order limits** to safeguard your entry and exit points. This can be done through:

Sell Limits: This involves setting a minimum value at which your shares will automatically be sold. This way, if the stock reaches that predetermined minimum, your shares will be sold without requiring constant monitoring.

Buy Limits: Here, you establish a maximum price at which you're willing to buy a share. This prevents you from having to constantly watch the position, as the purchase will be executed automatically once the stock hits your specified maximum price.

Naturally, in the realm of stock trading, there are various techniques for hedging through buying and selling. Feel free to explore more in-depth whenever you have the time. Last but not least, the two circles highlight the prime times to buy in for maximum gains with Company X and arrows show the potential gains. However, it's crucial to remember that this strategy comes with its own set of risks, as you're essentially purchasing while the stock is testing its support.

Yet, if you've diligently conducted your research and have a solid understanding of the company, seizing such an opportunity can work to your advantage. In considering the challenge of support levels and ceilings, this provides another avenue for analyzing these charts and leads us directly to our next topic – *patterns*.

Patterns

In this vast market, countless investors worldwide are vying for their share. Given that emotions are an integral part of human nature, relying solely on research, facts, and numbers may not be enough to navigate the challenges of this demanding environment. However, amidst the haze of emotions and the seemingly unpredictable movements of stocks, there emerges yet another valuable tool for us investors to employ – patterns. Patterns act as buy/sell signals and each stock possesses its distinct set of patterns; the key to discerning them lies in diligent research and vigilant market observation.

While patterns may not always be infallible, they hold global recognition among investors as an additional tool for gauging opportune buy or sell periods. Identifying patterns on stock charts isn't a straightforward task; it's much like searching for Waldo in a "Where's Waldo" book. The more you scrutinize the picture, the more likely you are to spot him eventually. Similarly, when it comes to stock patterns, the more time you invest in examining the charts, the more patterns will become apparent. While this may be challenging for beginners, with practice and experience, you'll start to discern patterns in every fluctuation of the chart! The realm of patterns is vast, but for now, let's focus on some simple, easy-to-spot patterns that you can capitalize on.

Double top

The double top pattern indicates that a stock has attempted to reach its ceiling twice but failed both times. This often signals an upcoming drop in the chart following the second unsuccessful attempt to break through the ceiling. **Double tops and double bottoms typically form an "M" shape pattern.**

Double bottom

The exact opposite of a double top pattern is a double bottom. In this case, the stock has tested its support level twice but failed to drop further. This usually indicates a rise in the stock's price after the second unsuccessful attempt to break the support level.

Teacup

In the teacup pattern, a "handle" emerges on the right side of the cup as a brief retracement following the significant upswing represented by the bear candlestick. After the completion of this handle, there is potential for the stock to experience a breakout, reaching new highs and establishing a new elevated price level as it resumes its regular trend.

Bear trending flag

The flag with a downward trend indicates that the stock is heading towards a bearish movement. This can be deduced by observing the consistent breaches of its support in a trending fashion. Generally, when the stock begins trading sideways and stabilizing, it is likely to recover and continue its previous uptrend.

Bull trending flag

The flag with a bull trend signifies a notable upward trend in a stock. This can be identified by the consistent breakthrough of its resistance level. However, due to the volatility and emotion-driven nature of the rise, the stock typically follows with a lower trend shortly thereafter.

It's now time to put this knowledge to the test and apply it in real-world scenarios. With this understanding, you should be able to discern specific situations in the market and take advantage of them. Begin by identifying the type of investor that aligns with your schedule. Next, conduct thorough research to select the type of stocks you wish to invest in. Once you've made your choice, closely monitor the chosen stock, conducting regular analysis and plotting. When you're ready, make your investment using stop losses/limits and then keep a close eye on the market, adjusting your strategy based on whether you're a daily, weekly, or monthly investor.

If you're feeling skeptical, take a step back and engage in market observation. Watch real-time data, analyze charts, observe patterns, and study stock behaviors based on their types. Take your time until you feel confident enough to start investing. If you're a beginner with limited capital, this is a prudent approach. Begin by trading with a small amount and once you consistently generate profits, gradually increase both your risk and capital. This way, you can build your confidence and skills over time.

Keep in mind that escalating risk necessitates adept portfolio hedging to minimize potential downsides. All of this information at once may seem a bit overwhelming, so let's take a step back in our next chapter and take a breather, to explore something that may not demand as much effort - something in the domain of... *passive investing.*

Your Best Friend - The Dividend!

A h yes, the dividend. You may or may not be familiar with this term, but it's frequently mentioned for good reason - dividends are a reliable ally for everyone. Let's redirect our attention to a company's earnings. When a company is profitable, it distributes a portion of those profits to its shareholders, these distributions are called dividends. Not to be confused with a stock's face value or its initial purchase price, a **dividend refers to a periodic payment (monthly, quarterly, semiannually, or annually) received for owning and holding a share**.

Consider this scenario: you acquire one share of ESS (ESSEX PROPERTY) at a face value of $220.80 per share. Additionally, the stock provides a quarterly dividend of $2.30 per share. This implies that if you possess fifty shares of ESS, you hold $11,040.00 in face value and receive $115.00 in passive income every three months for those fifty shares. That's an extra $460.00 in your pocket at the end of every year - not including the bullish(rises) or bearish(dips) of the stocks face value over the year.

Basically, when you hold a share that pays dividends, you're potentially gaining pure profit. In an ideal situation, the stock's face value is rising, and you're also receiving dividends on top of this increase, which further maximizes your gains. Depending on the sectors, companies will pay more or less dividends. For example, companies invested in natural resources typically pay higher dividends than those in sectors like food or technology. Hopefully, you're grasping the broader concept here. It's entirely possible and people have been doing it for years, to sustain oneself solely from just dividends.

There are individuals who have portfolios predominantly composed of companies offering substantial dividend yields, generating thousands, or even hundreds of thousands of dollars in dividends every year. Consider this perspective: When someone hears a friend or relative suggest, "You should give stock trading a try" they tend to envision themselves on their computer all day, actively managing their brokerage accounts, selling when prices are high and buying when they are low. In actuality, you can just consider the idea that you don't necessarily have to engage in active trading; simply holding onto them allows them to provide for you! I like to imagine laying back, smoking my cigar and letting that *sweet nectar* (passive income) flow in.

Bittersweet nectar

As sunny and upbeat as all of this sounds, in order to achieve the highest level of investment proficiency, we must also delve into the simple downsides and risks of dividend portfolios. However, rest assured, we shall also explore options and strategies to mitigate our risks. To begin, not all stocks issue dividends; shareholders must collectively vote in favor for a company to commence dividend payouts. Furthermore, it's important to note that not every dividend payment is guaranteed. Companies may fail to meet a distribution date due to revenue loss or a challenging business year. The face value of your dividend-paying stock can also be impacted if you opt for a high-yielding dividend stock that exhibits volatility.

This means that the face value price could fluctuate significantly in a relatively short span of time, to the extent that the dividend might not justify holding onto the stock. Occasionally, shareholders may decide to halt dividend payouts as a means to satisfy a specific segment of the shareholder community. Moreover, it's worth noting that establishing a prosperous, hands-off dividend portfolio may require a significant amount of capital. This is due to the challenge of identifying a consistently reliable, high-yielding dividend stock without firsthand experience and personal investment. *Okay, so how do I reliably hedge these risks and begin building a solid dividend portfolio?*

I'd like to begin by focusing on **high-yielding dividend stocks**. To put it plainly, this involves comparing the face value of a share to the annual dividends it pays out. For instance, take the company (T) AT&T. Currently, the face value of its shares is $14. They also pay a quarterly dividend of $0.28 per share. This equates to an 8 percent dividend yield per share, in a year, which is a rather favorable yield. Anything above 6 percent is generally considered quite high. This underscores the importance of opting for high-yielding dividend stocks, as they can offset the lower initial investment with their elevated yields.

Now, consider this: why would a company opt to increase its dividend yield, apart from factors like shareholder votes or overall company success? Well, one possible reason is to attract more shareholders, which could indicate that the company might be facing some challenges. Here's the scenario: a company in significant debt or facing financial difficulties may increase their dividend yield to attract more funding and stay afloat. While this might initially result in a high dividend yield for investors, there's a risk. If the company goes bankrupt, you could end up losing your entire position, potentially before the stock even pays out enough dividends to cover a significant portion of your costs. It's important to be cautious in such situations.

Your priority should be conducting thorough research to identify a stable stock that consistently provides a high dividend yield. Let's begin with kings and aristocrats – dividend kings and dividends aristocrats that is. A "**dividend aristocrat" is a stock that has upheld its promise of paying dividends for 25 years or more.** This is a substantial commitment, as dividends directly affect a company's net revenue. Hence, the company must have a track record of consistent profitability or resilience to sustain this practice for such an extended period. A "**dividend king" is even more remarkable. These are companies that have maintained a streak of 50 years or more of uninterrupted dividend payments**—an extraordinary achievement that demonstrates their enduring financial stability and success. To this day some of these kings are still afloat or even thriving.

Investing in dividend kings and aristocrats can be an excellent strategy for avoiding riskier, high-yield stocks. Interestingly, some of these aristocrats or kings also offer competitive yields. Remember to keep in mind that even dividend kings and aristocrats are still companies, which implies they are not immune to the possibility of no longer meeting the criteria for inclusion in these prestigious lists. Let's delve back into fund type stocks and how they tie into our next topic - dividend funds. Whether it's managed through a mutual fund or not, dividend funds, or income funds, primarily target sectors that generate income to help you establish a stream of passive income. They also provide a safer approach to passive dividend investing because you're exposed to multiple sectors globally, similar to any other fund. While they may not offer as high a yield as individual dividend stocks, they offer reliability and consistency.

Have you ever wanted to invest in real estate but lacked the initial capital? Well, you can get your foot in the door by using a crucial type of dividend-paying investment: **Real Estate Investment Trusts (REITs)**. These differ from regular equity stocks that offer high dividends. REITs are companies that invest in properties like apartment complexes or industrial buildings, which are then rented out to businesses or individuals. Essentially, you're providing the funding for the company's investments in additional properties or real estate ventures, and in return, you receive a portion of the rental income as dividends.

Personally, I have a fondness for REITs because they offer significantly higher dividend yields compared to regular equity stocks, and they also provide me with exposure to the real estate investment sector. Consider it as if you're putting your money into home mortgage loans and rental income without actually having to own or manage them yourself. It's a way to reap the benefits of the real estate market without the hands-on involvement. REITs do have some downsides to consider. Firstly, they can be directly affected by changes in interest rates.

If interest rates go up, companies or individuals may have a higher chance of missing their monthly payments, which could impact profits. Additionally, they have different tax implications compared to regular shares. It's crucial to conduct thorough research before making an investment in REITs. Given our newfound knowledge, let's create a theoretical dividend portfolio to help you grasp how it would function in practice. This exercise will provide a clearer mental image of the process.

To kick things off, I'd allocate 25 percent of my capital to REITs. They offer a higher degree of stability and aren't subject to the same level of scrutiny as regular companies in sectors outside of real estate. Next, I'd allocate another 25 percent to equity stocks that offer a solid, dependable yield. Unlike funds and REITs, the face value of equity stocks tends to be more volatile. This presents a great opportunity to sell in the future for potential gains, especially after capitalizing on dividends. Finally, the remaining 50 percent of my portfolio would be allocated to dividend funds, income funds, bond funds, and balance funds. These options also provide a reliable and steady stream of dividends, while offering exposure to various sectors globally, thereby minimizing potential losses in case of an economic downturn.

In the event of a crisis, my portfolio would essentially shift to a 50-50 allocation. For example, if my equity stocks, REITs, and funds were initially generating a steady passive income, but were negatively impacted by rising interest rates, my portfolio would then pivot towards the debt and commodities side. This means my bond funds and balance funds would provide a reliable source of profit, as they are diversified into assets like gold and other commodities that are less affected by market fluctuations. This strategy helps to cushion the impact of market downturns on my overall investment portfolio and just like that we have a basic outline for a solid dividend portfolio.

Think of it as a large balanced fund that you are managing, with 50 percent of assets in equity-generating stocks and the other 50 percent in assets outside of the stock market. Big business billionaires and millionaires employ this strategy because they have such substantial capital that it's akin to a savings account with an exceptionally high yield every year. For these individuals, we're talking about hundreds of thousands or even millions a year in passive income.

For many average investors, it's quite feasible to make thousands a year from dividends, eventually catching up with these millionaires and billionaires. *Combine this with your day, swing, position trading portfolio and you've successfully created an income-generating machine.*

CHAPTER 5

Leverage Trading

Insane gains, insane risk, extremely speculative. Depending on your capital investment, you can go from thousands to hundreds of thousands in a week. Certainly, it's essential to recognize that this involves a heightened level of risk – surpassing that of stocks. However, it's not accurate to equate leveraged trading with gambling. The approach to research and analysis for options is fundamentally distinct from that of traditional stock trading. Consider this chapter as a supplementary bonus, as options and leverage trading are geared towards more experienced traders. Given their close ties to stocks, I aim to provide a glimpse of their potential to inspire further exploration. I'll cover the basics of leverage trading, but the depth of understanding is something for you to explore on your own after further experience from the stock market.

To grasp leverage trading, it's essential to delve straight into options. Leverage trading and stock trading, while distinct, share a connection. Options serve as a form of leverage trading, intimately linked to stocks. When you acquire an **option, you're essentially obtaining a contract linked to stock shares.** This contract grants you the option (but not obligation) to buy or sell at or around its strike price before a specified expiration date. When purchasing this contract, you'll need to pay a **premium (a price cost for the contract)**, at the strike price. This **strike price serves as a wager on whether you believe the individual shares within the contract will reach that specified price.**

The premium is the fee you pay for the option contract, while the strike price represents your anticipated future value for the stock when the expiration date approaches. Additionally, the contract comes with an **expiration date, meaning the contract will be voided and no longer tradable after expiration.** This means you're essentially betting that the stocks linked to the contract will reach that price before it expires, or at least come close. This way, you can sell the contract to a buyer and reap the gains or buy all of the stock linked to the contract at the predicted price. The price of the contracts can vary widely based on the proximity of the stock price to the contract's strike price. This is quite different from individual company stocks, which usually only experience significant movement with major news or significant company developments.

Being near the strike price puts you "in the money," giving you the option to either **purchase all the shares in the contract (exercise)** at the strike price or sell the contract to someone else for a higher premium. However, this is only possible before the expiration date. If the contract reaches the expiration date and you're nowhere near your strike price, you lose the premium you paid for the contract (however much the contract costed). Most traders tend to trade contracts nearing their expiration date if they're in the money. However, if you have sufficient capital, you have the option to exercise the shares within the contract at the strike price, regardless of the current market value of the shares.

What does that mean? It means if you predicted a stock would reach $200 by the contract's expiration date, and the stock is sitting at $170, if it surpasses your prediction and reaches, let's say, $230 per share, you can purchase all the shares in the contract at $200 – your strike price. You'd be getting each share at a $30 discount due to your accurate market forecast. So, you see, options contracts essentially offer you the choice to buy or sell a stock once it reaches or exceeds the price you predicted. If you're wrong, you only lose the premium for the contract, not the shares inside it, since you never owned them in the first place, you just have the option to exercise but are not obligated to do so.

What you're really counting on when trading options are expiration dates, as the longer you hold them, the greater the chance of being in the money – here time will be your greatest ally or your enemy. Unfortunately, most options are extremely short term, typically weeks to couple months to maybe a few years max – although there are exceptions. You also have the amazing advantage of purchasing shares at a discounted rate if you're in the money by exercising, to enter into the market from your contract- the synergy between these elements operates so seamlessly.

Here's an incredibly simple example to illustrate:Picture yourself purchasing a box from Company A. This box is filled with, let's say, 100 sheets of paper. In this analogy, the box is akin to the options contract offered by Company A, and the paper inside it represents 100 shares of Company A within that box. You pay $100 as a premium for the box. The box has a strike price of $200, while each sheet of paper inside is valued at $170. This box expires in one week. In five days, the value of the sheets inside the box increases to $250, thanks to a breakthrough in Company A's sales. The box's price remains at $200 (strike price), and the premium jumps up to $200.

At this point, you have the option to sell the box, making a $100 profit. Alternatively, you can choose to exercise the box, buying the 100 sheets of paper inside for $170 each, a significant discount from their current market price of $250. This resembles traditional stock trading, but with the added dimension of trading contracts that grant the option to buy shares within that contract. It's fairly straightforward. However, here's where the significant divergence of leveraged trading becomes evident: you have the ability to profit from a stock's decline by betting against it, a feature not present in regular stock purchases.

The real beauty of leverage trading lies in the ability to use options to amplify the impact of your stocks in the market. Consider the earlier example with the box and sheets of paper, where we bet on an upswing. Now, imagine reversing that scenario, and it works just the same way, but this time, you're wagering on a market downturn. Since options are contracts and don't entail actual ownership of shares, you have the potential to profit from a market downturn. This is because options become more valuable as they approach their strike price, whether that strike price is betting on the market to go down OR up! Let me give you a quick example: say you own shares of Company B, but you're concerned that the company's upcoming earnings report might lead to a significant drop in the stock price. To safeguard your position in the stock market, you decide to purchase an options contract, speculating on a potential downturn. This way, if your stock does indeed drop significantly, the proceeds from selling the contract can help offset some of the losses. If you were anticipating an upturn, you'd opt for a call option. However, if you're betting on a downturn, you'd go for a put option.

Call Option:

Buyer's Perspective: A call option gives the buyer the right (but not the obligation) to buy a specific asset (like a stock) at a predetermined price (the strike price) before or on the expiration date of the option.

Seller's Perspective: The seller (writer) of the call option is obligated to potentially sell the asset to the buyer if the buyer decides to exercise the option.

Put Option:

Buyer's Perspective: A put option gives the buyer the right (but not the obligation) to sell a specific asset (like a stock) at a predetermined price (the strike price) before or on the expiration date of the option.

Seller's Perspective: The seller (writer) of the put option is obligated to potentially buy the asset from the buyer if the buyer decides to exercise the option.

In both cases, the buyer pays a price (called the premium) to the seller for the option. This premium is the cost of obtaining the right to buy (in the case of a call option) or sell (in the case of a put option) the underlying asset at the agreed-upon price. Remember, options trading involves risks and may not be suitable for all investors. It's important to understand the potential outcomes and consult with a financial advisor if you're considering participating in options markets. Now that you've grasped the basics of options, let me introduce you to something that might have been somewhat overlooked: Employee Stock Options (ESOs). Remember when I mentioned exceptions to short expiration dates? ESOs are a prime example of this.

If you're in the market for a 9 to 5 job, or already have one, it's crucial to delve into your company's benefits package. Nowadays, many companies provide perks like stock rewards, and one such offering is Employee Stock Options (ESOs). Essentially, they function just like regular options, but come with a considerably longer expiration period. This is like striking gold since as a primary drawback of regular options is their limited lifespan. Having more time is advantageous, but most options have too brief an expiration window. ESOs, on the other hand, typically remain valid for a whopping 10 years. This extended duration is exceptionally favorable for potentially lucrative investments. Options are mainly a risk because of their volatility and time factor.

Volatility is directly correlated to time, as over time a stock will have more chances to correct its volatility. Though rare if your company offers this, personally I would jump at the opportunity instantly. Consider a real-world example: when Facebook (now META) initially launched, they provided their employees with stock options that had a notably lengthy expiration date. Naturally, these options were vested gradually over time to ensure that employees remained committed to the company and didn't simply cash out and depart. Given Facebook's current status as a multi-billion-dollar enterprise, one can only fathom the staggering value of those Employee Stock Options (ESOs) in today's market. This is precisely why there are numerous individuals who formerly worked for Facebook during its startup phase and have now achieved multi-millionaire status.

Equally, it's crucial to acknowledge a significant distinction. Due to the time sensitivity of options and their distinct behavior compared to stocks, traditional news and media research may not provide reliable insights -unless, your option is from several months to years. When dealing with shorter-term options, it's more effective to approach them with a mindset akin to scalping or swing trading. Rely on patterns and chart data rather than emotional reactions or extensive research into company financials and numerical data. Options trading is a vast topic, almost deserving of its own guide. The key message here is to actively pursue different trading opportunities and capitalize on them.

In addition to options, there are also leveraged funds, as mentioned in Chapter 1. These funds allow you to wager on market movements, whether up or down, similar to contracts. However, instead of buying individual stocks, you're investing in funds that hold a portfolio of companies engaged in options contracts. This provides a different avenue for leveraging your investments. We're constantly surrounded by potential avenues like this, but our ability to seize them was once constrained by a lack of comprehension. You've merely skimmed the surface; plunge into the depths of options. *Seek counsel from financial sages or embark on a voyage of diligent research, for here, the chance to transcend from pauper to prince, or from prince to pauper, holds no prejudice.*

CHAPTER 6

Ready?

Before we disembark on our journey together and you set off to leverage your recently acquired knowledge, I'd like to take a moment to shift our focus away from stocks and touch on a few more aspects of income in a broader sense. Much like many dedicated, industrious individuals, I'm always on the lookout for additional avenues of revenue, as my aspirations extend to building prosperity for the generations to come. Keep in mind, wealth is gauged by time, while riches are quantified in monetary terms. During your journey, you'll encounter various obstacles along the way. However, how you handle these challenges will ultimately shape your success as a trader.

Never allow fear to dictate your decisions. Instead, prioritize research to bolster your confidence in the field. Remember, confidence isn't innate; it's cultivated through making composed and rational choices in the face of fear. Our minds define our boundaries, and our knowledge is confined until we expand it, unlocking fresh potential and opportunities that we can then seize upon. With that said, I'd like to elaborate on various avenues for generating income. Here, I present a range of compelling methods, both passive and active, that can be integrated into your *income-generating machine.*

Real estate investing – While it demands substantial initial capital and entails a challenging start, venturing into real estate unlocks one of the most potent avenues for generating passive income in the long run.

Royalties – Are you familiar with royalties? It's a passive income stream where you receive payment for any music, artwork, or creations you produce, and companies have to compensate you for using or distributing your product. Ever been in Walmart or Target and heard the background ambience? Well, the person who created that track is earning a substantial amount every day from stores playing their music.

CDS – Certificates of deposits, or CDs, are similar to savings accounts but offer higher interest rates. The only drawback with CDs is that you can't withdraw funds until a specific period, similar to bonds. While the yields may not be as remarkable as those from trading dividend stocks, CDs are widely regarded as a secure investment option, providing a higher level of safety compared to stocks.

Sell a product – Whether you're utilizing ecommerce to sell products online or conducting physical sales in a store, it all boils down to the age-old principle of supply and demand. As long as there are people on this planet, the desire for goods is inherent. Identify what the majority is currently seeking and seize the opportunity! Immerse yourself in the intricacies of shipping and delve into the dynamic world of buying and selling!

Embarking on a business venture - especially one centered around selling a product, is a substantial undertaking. It's not as straightforward as merely starting a business. It involves a degree of risk, unless you possess a solid grasp of business operations, management, economics, and the principles of supply and demand. However, if successful, a business can offer one of the highest returns on investment. Moreover, if your business evolves into a corporation, you can avail yourself of significant tax advantages!

Cryptocurrency – Now, this is a highly debated subject. Although it comes with significant risks and is reminiscent of peer-to-peer trading, there's a reason why cryptocurrencies persist and have stood the test of time. Venturing into the world of crypto can almost feel rebellious, given that it challenges traditional government-backed currencies.

Why? Because cash or the dollar represents a government's monetary reserves, and treasuries have authority over the dollar. Gold is often seen as a form of 'divine money,' a natural resource deemed valuable and unreplaceable. On the other hand, crypto is considered 'people's money'- decentralized, beyond government regulation or control. Hopefully, this has piqued your curiosity enough to delve deeper. Consider this: when you visit official government sites for purchasing gold and silver bullion, isn't it intriguing that they accept most cryptocurrencies as payment? I'll leave you with that, a little food for thought.

High-yield savings accounts - are essentially bank savings accounts that allow you to withdraw funds at your convenience, similar to a standard savings account. The key distinction lies in their significantly higher interest rates, akin to certificates of deposit (CDs). However, it's worth noting that CDs typically offer only a slightly higher interest rate compared to a high-yield savings account. It's advisable to shop around, as different banks provide varying interest rates and may require you to apply before opening an account.

Creating videos for online entertainment - has become increasingly popular. In today's tech-savvy era, people are glued to screens, whether it's on the internet or television. The entertainment industry has been flourishing for as long as I can recall. If you possess excellent editing skills, you can tap into this trend to attract viewers and generate income.

Sponsorship Advertising- is a versatile method that can complement any of the business strategies mentioned earlier. For instance, you can earn revenue by allowing companies to run ads on your online platforms, be it websites or videos. This serves as a valuable addition to your passive income stream, akin to the steady income a royalty provides.

Advancing in your 9-5 job - is a crucial step in the quest for increased income. While many aspire to early retirement, it's important to recognize that your 9-5 job provides a dependable and consistent source of income at present. This income is the foundation for building your capital for future investments; it's where you secure your "employees". Therefore, opt for a 9-5 role that offers ample benefits and opportunities for both financial and personal growth. Remember, in this setting, you have a structured path for professional development.

Invest in physical precious metals and gems- In a scenario that might be considered more apocalyptic, where the worst-case unfolds, such as the potential destruction of the civil world leading to the devaluation or disappearance of any country's currency, the reliance would shift back to trading in precious commodities. This practice has ancient roots, as humans discovered the enduring value of substances like gold and gems thousands of years ago.

Their worth has consistently appreciated over time. Consider how gold is often turned to as a hedge against the dollar during economic downturns, given its ancient and enduring value. Furthermore, metals like platinum, gold, and silver play critical roles in everyday applications, serving as conductors for electricity and refined materials for construction. They essentially underpin various aspects of our world, and most precious metals and gems cannot be replicated by human effort, solidifying their status as assets of intrinsic value. Nevertheless, holding physical gold and silver can be cumbersome, requiring secure storage and protective measures. One other downside is that gold and silver lack the same level of liquidity as the dollar, particularly when it comes to the thriving of the economy.

Armed with the insights gained from this book, you now possess the tools to navigate various financial avenues. It's imperative to choose your path wisely. Now, you're on a level playing field with the banks and the federal institutions. You've been instructed on the skill of keeping your capital active by capitalizing on stocks and dividends, discerning their trends. This knowledge empowers you to amass greater wealth.

You've also learned about the diverse methods of investment and the various stock types that permeate the market thus generating income. Additionally, you've been equipped with strategies to shield your wealth from inflation through market hedging techniques, including leverage and debt instruments. Embarking on your investment journey, it's crucial to exercise prudence. Begin with a measured pace and a modest approach. As profits start to materialize, resist the urge to succumb to greed - a pitfall that has led many astray. Greed can blind traders and erode their sense of caution and risk management. Instead of hedging their funds, they may choose to pour all their capital into high-returning stocks, only to suffer significant losses when adversity strikes.

Remember, steady and considered progress often yields the most sustainable results. Do not allow your own mindset to impose limitations on your potential. Keep seeking additional avenues to grow your wealth. You've already taken a crucial step that many overlook - choosing to invest your money rather than simply spending it. You understand that in the long, or even possibly the short run, you'll not only recoup your investment but potentially gain even more. This forward-thinking approach is the foundation of prosperous financial management.

Stock trading encompasses a vast body of knowledge that is closely intertwined with business, economics, and finance. Broadening your understanding of these fields will significantly enhance your ability to excel in stock trading. Therefore, invest time in studying these domains, as it will undoubtedly contribute to your success in the world of stock trading. With newfound wisdom, you unveil the hidden truths, revealing a world beyond your wildest imaginings. *May fortune favor your journey, investor, and may your investments dance with prosperity!*

GLOSSARY

Principle - Funds agreed to be paid back.

Defaulting - Company fails to issue payments towards its debts or files for bankruptcy.

Capital - Any wealth, in form of assets or money used for the purpose of investing.

Equity - Total net worth after liquidating all assets.

Premium - Amount initially paid for acquiring an asset.

Derivative - Financial contracts that are valued depending on an underlying asset.

Hedge - Adressing future risks by insuring them with a plan and strategies.

Offset - Opposite reaction.

Subsidary - A secondary Company that is owned by a parent company.

Vest/Vesting - A time period of waiting until you are able to take full ownership of an asset.

Security - Anything with monetary value.

Collateral - Used to offset losses or insure an asset.

Bull - Positive, rises.

Bear - Negative, dips.

Volatility - Price movement of an asset.

Face value - Current Initial purchase price.

Volume - Quanitity being traded.

Strike price - price of a security that can be bought or sold once exercised.

Exercise - Act of buying or selling all securities within a financial contract.

Stock Funds - Basket of securities.

Portfolio - Collection of financial assets such as stocks, bonds and other securities held by investors.

Broker - A person or firm that facilitates the buying and selling of financial securities on behalf of investors.

Price to earnings ratio - A financial ratio that measures a company's current share price relative to its per-share earnings.

Margin - Borrowed funds used to invest into securities.

Blue Chip Stocks - Stocks of large, well established, and financially sound with a history of stable performance.

Spread - Difference between the bid and ask prices of a security. It represents the transaction cost for buying and selling.

Dividend - A portion of a company's earnings distributed to its shareholders, usually in the form of cash or more shares.